G̲agaan X̲'usyee
Below the Foot of the Sun

ALASKA LITERARY SERIES

Peggy Shumaker, Series Editor

**ALASKA
LITERARY
SERIES**

The Alaska Literary Series publishes poetry, fiction, and literary
nonfiction. Successful manuscripts have a strong connection to
Alaska or the circumpolar north, are written by people living in the far
north, or both. We prefer writing that makes the northern experience
available to the world, and we choose manuscripts that offer
compelling literary insights into the human condition.

G̱agaan X̱'usyee

Below the Foot of the Sun

X̱'unei Lance Twitchell

University of Alaska Press FAIRBANKS

© 2024 by University Press of Colorado

Published by University of Alaska Press
An imprint of University Press of Colorado
1580 North Logan Street, Suite 660
PMB 39883
Denver, Colorado 80203-1942

 The University Press of Colorado is a proud member of
Association of University Presses.

The University Press of Colorado is a cooperative publishing enterprise
supported, in part, by Adams State University, Colorado State University,
Fort Lewis College, Metropolitan State University of Denver, University of
Alaska Fairbanks, University of Colorado, University of Denver, University
of Northern Colorado, University of Wyoming, Utah State University, and
Western Colorado University.

∞ This paper meets the requirements of the ANSI/NISO Z39.48-1992
(Permanence of Paper).

ISBN: 978-1-64642-554-9 (hardcover)
ISBN: 978-1-64642-555-6 (paperback)
ISBN: 978-1-64642-556-3 (ebook)
https://doi.org/10.5876/9781646425563

Cataloging-in-Publication data for this title is available online at the Library of
Congress

Cover art by X̱'unei Lance Twitchell

For Miriah.

*Our paths crossed in 2006, and since that time we have
made the most wonderful rope out of our two lives, which
became five with Kiana, Ava, and Ḵájaa. I am so grateful
to you all. You showed me love I thought unattainable.*

Contents

TRANSLATIONS

Shóogunáx̱

Acknowledgments

This collection spans decades, but it never would have come together without the support of my wonderful life partner, Miriah Twitchell. Through our years of outdoor adventures and travel, she has constantly looked for opportunities for me to work on creative, language, and academic projects by finding residencies and funding opportunities and by encouraging me to find time in our busy lives as parents of fabulous and busy children. Her love comforts me, and her courage helps me take steps when I hesitate. We go on adventures and she constantly provides opportunities to try new things, go new places, and find times to focus on finishing projects.

Poetry sometimes takes forever. This collection includes poems that were written in the late 1990s, in the early days of my journey as a poet, and some that were written in 2023. This collection and these poems have experienced racism just as I have, and they have experienced kindness just as I have. A few of my poetry teachers over these decades were Diane Glancy, Derick Burleson, Amber Flora Thomas, and some of my fiction teachers were Julie Schumacher, David Crouse, and Gerri Brightwell. There have been many others, and also many colleagues who were there when these poems were being written and work-shopped, and many of them shared their incredible work with me as well. This collection was reviewed with love by Peggy Shumaker, who has supported me as a writer for over a decade. I am thankful to Christopher Lee Miles, who encouraged me to dust it off and send it around, and to Don Rearden, who supported me through times of engaging with editorial racism.

"When the Heart Skips a Beat" and "Sable Voices" were published in *Ice Box* (2010). "Nanook Sweats," "Release,

Definition: Trickster," "Ode to Tlingit," and "Dark Skin and Be-traying Uncle" were published in *Yellow Medicine Review* (Spring 2009). "Shux'wáa Yoo X̱'atángi" was woven into a beautiful poem by Emily Wall, "Shaawatk'é's Birth," which was published in her book *Breaking into Air* (2022) and was also published in the *Alaska Quarterly Review* and made into a short film to cele-brate the thirty-fifth anniversary of the journal (2017).

This book was developed with assistance from an Individual Artist Fellowship from the Rasmuson Foundation (2021), an artist residency at Headlands Center for the Arts (2018), a resi-dency at Alderworks Alaska Writers and Artists Retreat (2017), a Connie Boochever Fellowship in the literary and performing arts (2013), and scholarships from the Vine Deloria Jr. Memo-rial Scholarship at the American Indian College Fund (2009), Native Forward Scholars Fund, Sealaska Heritage Institute, the CIRI Foundation, and Central Council of Tlingit and Haida Indian Tribes of Alaska.

I am grateful to my mentors who inspired me while they were alive, in particular Derick Burleson, Nora Dauenhauer, Richard Dauenhauer, George Davis, Marge Dutson, and Cyril George. Colleagues who inspire and teach creative writing deserve a ton of credit, especially Emily Wall and Ernestine Saankalaxt' Hayes, who reminded me regularly to stay creative. Jonas Lamb gave the manuscript a wonderful and encouraging review, and Maria Shaa Tláa Williams has always been a won-derful academic advocate and mentor.

X̱eixwnéi Nora Marks Dauehnauer and Sol Neely were ex-traordinary partners in decolonial shenanigans. Nora came up with the word «at shí yoo x̱'atánk» (song language) for poetry, and Sol was my chief strategist in figuring out how to be kind while continually trying to change a cruel colonial world.

Gunalchéesh!

For the Translanguagers

We often live between multiple languages and perspectives, and if you do not currently speak Lingít, this section seeks to ground you in a few important concepts. This collection is divided into four parts, based on how we talk about gagaan (the sun).

Gagaan x'oos is literally "sun's foot" and is the term we use to talk about a sunbeam. Gagaan x'usyee is "below the foot of the sun" and is used to talk about a ray of sunlight that bursts through the clouds. Gagaan x'us.eetí is "remains of the foot of the sun" and is the name we use for a patch of sunlight on the ground or floor. Gagaan xanyádi is "child next to the sun" and is our word for a sundog. These four sections are arranged emotionally and begin or end with a series of poems that I wrote in New Mexico when touring Navajo country and was trying to write a novel that would take place there. In these sections, a southern trickster, Coyote, breaks through the text to share a set of songs that are poems.

A glossary of the Lingít used in this text can be found in the appendix. One reviewer of this text said my use of Lingít without translation felt like outdated politics of the 1970s. They said other unkind things about my work, but that just means it is not for them and their monolingual constrictions.

Gunalchéesh for engaging. Gunalchéesh for translanguaging. Gunalchéesh for dancing with tricksters. Gunalchéesh for hearing the echoes of those I knew in this world and will recognize in the next.

G̲agaan X̲'usyee
Below the Foot of the Sun

G̲agaan X̱'oos

Coyote Song I

Imprints of claws   on a cool riverbank
—proof of my thirst for the world—
and I come   back & back   back & back   again because
 people of the red clay need to hear songs
about eternity,   consume it like feast born into the honor
 beat
of their   new   Ghost Dance.

Yes, I have a nose for trouble, flinching.
Yes, I was born beneath the desert, screaming.
Yes, there is a heaven for mothers and daughters built by
 strong sons and fathers.

In that place we call strength.

Woolnáx̱ Wooshk̲ák̲[*]

for K̲áalaa Miriah Twitchell

Those little birds go full speed into their home.
Raven named them "landed through a hole,"
and I watch, amazed at their precision.

You and I are just the right touch of chaos,
emerging from battery and booze and drugs,
creating home for these babies who are you, me, us.

An Unangan man once talked about watching
seabirds: a mass of thousands moving,
impossible fast yet never colliding.

The image keeps surfacing in my mind:
I first saw you hauling luggage off the belt,
I watched longer than I should have, but that was you.

He said those seabirds are a combined organism,
constant motion that relies on instinct,
watching them is meditation: bird cloud.

Life scratches around us, leaving new scars.
I nuzzle hills and valleys, twists and turns
that push me to oblivion.

---

[*] The Tlingit name for a wren, which translates to "landed through a hole."

4

Among the hemlock, citrus breaks the mouth,
a bird that flies without sound moves between trees,
when they choose another it is for life.

These birds and their nests. I wonder about which worlds
they maintain, how I told you this time is forever,
and we rise and fall like love tides.

Sable Voices

I hear your words and whispers,
they are thick like oatmeal,
with razor images that tumble
from the might of your wisdom.

You are the sum of our knowledge,
which explains your trickery,
why we can only understand you
by peering into our hearts.

I see your stories and troubles,
they are rich with color;
we try to recall the grace in
our everyday motions and dancing.

You are the black of my ink,
whispering all your latest tricks.

Listening without understanding,
I follow the beauty of your voice.

Irrational

The table and chair have lost
   their place in the kitchen.

   Falsetto conversation begins
when rage first fills the air,
   one ear prepares for sudden flight
when the violence erupts,
   shatters the fragile wooden chair,
rumbles down the stairway
   with the stench of bourbon, ashtrays,
vomit and perspiration
   piggybacking the coming attack.

A room
   confines vertigo.

   Sporadic sleep takes this child
to a landscape where raindrops
   wash the bruised surface,
scent of wet earth, mist of security
   coats the calming sea.

Madness has become
   a rationed substance.

   The backyard has become
an assortment of household objects
   and the family has fallen to sleep
in pieces.

Óosk'i Aa[*]

Kaséixjaa Kiana Catherine Twitchell

ax óosk'i aa.
x'alitseeni át.
ilikoodzée.
ax yádi.

i gu.aa yáx x'wán.
i gu.aa yáx x'wán.

wáanganeens
galadzéech áwé yá Lingít'aaní.

gwál yé
tlél uk'éiyi aa yáx kaaxát
yá Lingít'aaní.

tlél haa aayí áwé ch'a ldakát át.

Haa Aaní.
Haa Kusteeyí.
Haa Yoo X'atángi.

a ku.aa i tóo yéi yatee,
haa tutáni.

kagaxtoo.aakw, tsú kagaxtoo.aakw
has du tundatáanix

---

* An English translation of this poem appears on page 95.

haa guxsatée
Haa Tlagu Ḵwáanx'i Yán.

has du toowú latseeníx̱.
isitee

ax̱ yádi.
ilikoodzée.
x̱'alitseeni át.
ax̱ óosk'i áa.

Killer Whale Like a Person Sewing

for Ḵaalḵéis' Kiana Twitchell

There was a time when language was finding its home,
and I began to dream in Lingít.
Your father's mother's father's mother was there.
    I had been wandering after a rope broke,
      and I had drifted downstream on the current.

She tossed pictures of Raven to the ground,
then looked at me and said: yéi áwé aadé yéi yoo dudzineigi
    yé.

But did I know it then like I do now, or was she an act
of translation for me, knowing that you would be coming?
They say the old people could see way out into the future
    through our language, and she had already
      entered the dreams of my mother's mother.

These lines, my child, they are etched into the earth,
connecting us to place, time, each other.

These strings of land, island, peninsula, water,
they are places where Eternal Ones found homes for us,
we care for future generations by weaving
    a cedar bark mat that waits
      for next occupant.

My teacher Shgaté placed one of her names on you,
and through that she and you became my daughters.

She said the killer whales, when they travel in a pod
—kéet x̱áa yaa nagwéin—have one at the front,
rising and falling, creating its own tide,
    like a person sewing,
    black and white piercing seawater.

I knew you when I saw you,
walking back into a life we share.

Definition: Trickster

for Derick Burleson

A man asked me today: what is a trickster anyway?
What is Raven? A god? An angel? A prophet?
I found trifle and tribune in a pocket dictionary,
began humming the tune of a trail song brought
back in a sack with beaver pelts and moose meat.
Drifted to a dream in which the caribou fell like
wooden matches balanced upright in high winds.
Waited for their screams but in the eerie silence saw the
wanton waste and the rotted meat, calves milking dead
    mothers,
I long for a cup of coffee with my papa.

Raven turns upon itself. The definition thickens like years old
oil, black with use and littered with metallic flakes that tell of
a coming breakdown, of wear and war and waste. The river
is an odd mixture of silt and salt, blood and bourbon, scars
and laughter. I drift to a dream where flames lick up to the
    top
of my favorite carvings, the markers that show which land
    belongs
to which clan. A young man shoots the top of his own clan
    marker,
his face is a riddle of pockmarks where we trade smallpox for
    influenza,
tuberculosis for meth, ceremony for distance.

Standing amongst the raindrops that come incessantly in
    sideways

patterns, I toil through the pages in hopes that the answer is
    there—
why Raven could release fresh water, salmon, stars and
    daylight, and
then seemingly leave us to our own disastrous methods. I let
    the small
book fall into the river, it floats off like a canoe without a
    rudder,
a man without wisdom, the echo of a shape that does not
    exist,
is not carved from the soil and dripping with blood and
    suffering.

The voice comes up from the river.
The voice comes up from the river.
It is distant at first, the sound of other footfalls while walking
through a dense forest, a beaver pushing rocks off the shore.
Definitions turn upon themselves to reveal nothing but the
    paint-
stripped surface of an old carving, one that has survived fires
    and floods,
its children turning upon themselves and their people.

The man has been here long enough to answer his own
    question,
beginning with a riddle of silence. I look into his eyes and see
    my distorted reflection.
This is stillness. The river roars into my ear all the things I
    could say—

the history of a people who have lost their way over and over
    again.
It is a pattern, I tell him. One that comes from your mind,
imitation of imitation, trying to mimic the voice of the river,
pretending to be ourselves.

It is a man being eaten by cancer and laughing and loving
    because his
footprint is filled with joy and faith and the language of his
    paternal uncles.
It is the hammer nose that carved a place for us where we
    were born,
in the lap of our paternal aunties. It is all of this and none of
    this and more.
It is the soft call of one solitary Raven who has lost her loved
    one.
And she will not stop looking. It is the voice of reason in a
    time of pestilence.
It is the voice of the spirit that left luggage and dryfish
    bundles in a river that
fills with sustenance year in and year out.

It is never too late, I tell him, to start our own definition.

Shux'wáa Yoo X̱'atángi*

Shaawatk'é Ava Renae Twitchell

ax̱ yádi.
ax̱ yádi.

i eegáa ḵuwtuwashee
i eegáa ḵuwtuwashee

wéidu i tláa
i tláa áwé

x̱át áyá i éesh
gunalchéesh
gunalchéesh

ch'a yéi gunéin
tlax̱ lidzée yá ḵustí haa jeex̱
haa yoo x̱'atángi yaa nanáan

a ḵu.aa i een áyá
kei gux̱latseen
kei gux̱latseen

haa Lingítx̱ sateeyí

woosh tudzix̱án
haa yoo x̱'atángi tin

---

* An English translation of this poem appears on page 97.

woosh tudzix̲án
haa yoo x̲'atángi tin

gunalchéesh, gunalchéesh
yéi áwé

Lovelike War

I wish to crawl beneath your concrete bandages
where no one can steal our reclaimed innocence.

In peace we are the poultice,
we are nectar-drawing hummingbirds,
nesting in erotic comfort and feeding on life.

But love glaciates, immobile and ungiving,
learns to untrust, feeds the chasm until it grows,
and we turn tadpoles to demigods.

Yet you nuzzle inside my trouble,
planting lilacs on a landscape torn to rubble
from a nurturing that tasted like bourbon,
like a sharp metallic realization of blood
in your mouth, spilling onto a
cold & clammy cement floor.

    In the tree—Raven—stops calling.

He turns the other way, from whitecaps on a cold sea
to deeply wooded coasts of Oregon, where the Creator's
    Fingers
cut rocks to the shore, where in a mist of hazel
fragrant beach greens & rhythmic pounding breathe salty
    life.

The easy lines read whispers that permeate honeysuckle,
but we are the struggle between, residing in corners

where failure births the crackle of crushed wrists
stripped of cartilage and strength.

Beyond these rugged hills morning dew renews,
fresh dirt in a fine mist of rain, that scent of spirit helpers.
Turning over and over again in your tide,
I watch as the bold face of the Sun enriches, frightens, burns
    to roots.

Earthquake Poems

TREPIDATION

Yaa kanagwátl yá Lingít'aaní.
This world is spinning.

Think about a stopping point,
or even a pause, when the oscillation
might give way to stillness.

I close my eyes and count between
the tremors, hesitate to let out a breath
in hopes that my motion is linked.

The limbs of the trees hold no snow,
and the days reach their ends
as we tremble yet again.

Hounded by Wolves

For the UAF MFA Cohort

I know the lid on the mason jar,
dented with intention, this pack of hands
secure within, fingers mashed together
bound by whispers, shedding secret.

I know the sun sets thirty days north
of the arctic circle, and left to my deeds,
vices, wish for falling Eagle down, ceremony
with tin can lodges smoldering papers.

I know the institute of repetition seeks
a new rendition of these, our favorite
hidden voices, whose faded footfalls
are scratches filled of pen and ink.

I know hours when voices from the wall threaten
to whiten the page, tiny vessels fishtail
youth for splendor, subject, timbre as
knuckles flounder a trusted toolbox.

I know no other place for solitary confinement
where waitresses, voodoo, games, mushrooms
turn dust to gold, old dogs clap time while bracelets
and nightmare bears cut the hills of Montana.

I know words along the subsurface.
What odor is that reverie?
And every word spoken aloud sounds
less like apples and more like paint chips.

I know you because you know ice crystals
on my breath taste of freshly peeled birch bark.
We chase our tails for that dead dog bite,
line within line, voices transcend into time.

Raven's Sugarbowl

Gooshdehéen Si Dennis Sr.

With my grandfather, everything is sugar.
Folgers with can milk and three teaspoons.

Frozen blueberries congealing all.

He tells me stories over stories,
running over my words.
My mouth hangs open,
ready to give something interesting, important.

More sugar. Sweet creamy coffee.

Now I drink it black,
but the sweetness is still there,
ready to hear all I've finally learned to say.

Breath Like a Drum

L Tuwax̱sée Dorothy Dennis

A text message informed me our time was limited.
I remember how breath vacated my body,
    I read it over and over,
    must have read it wrong.

In Anchorage there was distinct chaos,
an uprising against your caretaker, my mother,
    the diagnoses could not be heard,
    some thought more could be done to keep you.

The doctor said some things, but I remember
the word liquified and knew we had to get you home:
    this is where you always wanted to be,
    our beloved gumboot who weathered any tide.

The flag on Uncle's house threw patterns from the wind,
you said a lot of people were coming, a big party,
    Uncle Paulie was cooking salmon.
    They came for your journey.

I had four songs picked out for you, two Haida for us,
two Lingít for your husband and children,
    grandchildren lined up, great-grandchildren
    closing tiny hands on your memory.

The last one was our cry song. We had all gathered.
I held your hand. And when the last vocable left my mouth
    your body rocked and gave its final breath,
    a drum echoed in valleys where we were orphaned.

G̲agaan X̱'usyee

Coyote Song II

Grandmother
I hear your new song,
calling out to me from
inside a cavern,
and the VCR of my mind
plays a loop of rattles and water drums.

Grandfather
I hear your new story,
peeling thick hide from my skin,
replacing it with an outer shell
warm and soft, full of
Grandmother's beautiful chant,
made with darkened hands
that protect me
from all the world

All the world.

If Jesus Were a Basketball Player

He would play the low post
where the team's dirty work
wins ball games
taking elbows from the opposition
while establishing position in
dusty, buckled Air Jerusalems.

Moses would have a mean crossover,
earning him a position at off-guard.

Coach could play Adam at center—
men love the middle of attention.

Mary could run at small forward,
scoring from the outside.

And I'm sure Coach would
place Eve at the point;
He's seen what happens
when a man runs the team.

The Old Lady with All the Money

This gallery is all dust and façade,
planted in a town where gold rush
is the center of humanity,
trapping us in a place of false beginnings.

There was a world that wasn't coated in snow.

An old lady walks in and makes the rounds,
she picks a mask off the wall like it's an insect,
gritting rows of opercula, a shade of bluish-green
that has taken a lifetime of practice to perfect.

It's called "Warrior with a Stroke" but I don't tell her that.

The mask is made of alder, dried out and on its way
to anciently familiar, half its face wrinkled and sagging,
pupils rolled up in a way that symbolizes visions
of a world populated with spirit helpers, living dead.

We are all foreigners to the familiar.

Her face pulls down at the edges so much
I picture a white rat perched on her hand,
scratching towards her face with its pink eyes
and pink tail—it brings a plague of devices.

My grandfather's grandparents are buried in the hills here.

This town is a row of buildings designed to look old,
tenants hunger for the dollars of the same tourists
who shop the same stores in the Caribbean winter,
a traveling world of illusions that has taken over.

The rush never quit, merciless in its consumption.

She finally asks why these masks are so expensive:
"I bought one just like this in the Philippines for five
dollars, and you expect me to pay a thousand here?
Can you tell me why?" she asks, oblivious.

"Natives like money, too," I tell her, and watch her walk
out the door, taking all that she has somewhere else,
where stolen lies can shake hands over bones forgotten.

The First Real Pain

A boy and his dog.

Makes me think
Norman Rockwell,
except this picture
has more darkness,
harsh brush strokes
from a demon of an artist.

May God forgive,
he is killing the dog.

The boy is a failure,
which will make the
madman a murderer.

A boy and his dog.

Survivors,
veterans of a war
on whiskey.

The dog is sore,
but not broken.

He is stronger than he looks.

The boy wears
bruises on the inside,
they will not heal.

He is stronger than he looks.

When the Heart Skips a Beat

Just ask the Natives about Christian love,
they'll tell of times when devils rode along
the sacred backs of their grandparents' land
and dashed the innocence of children like
a vole in the mouth of a rattlesnake,
of times when the words of their ancestors
were smashed against the rocks where Coyote
once danced with a hunter's precision,
this is only the beginning of story,
the place where blood-cracked beginnings are born.

The children's voices echo like a ghost
where broken men arise from broken men,
and everywhere there are answers within
riddles where Raven tosses round black stones
into the river, like his luggage, like
his dryfish bundle, and his women are
hungered, and her children are disciples
of massacred souls, and let it end, these
meals of ash where no songs wait to carry
us like pods in the stream where salmon spawn
instead of rot in the mold of neglect.
And I wish I told you sooner, Papa,
and I wish I sang it sooner, Náanii,
but now we stand in fits of mud and grass
with scales and eggs spoiled between wrinkled toes.

Earthquake Poems

DEAR MOTHER

It's been a minute
since the world shifted.
These walls, they bear the weight,
shift in time with earth beat.

They say the ground can ripple,
the tide at one point reached
its apex and Raven sent
his mother into this little bird.

You float upon the waves,
nothing is going to happen.
You float upon the waves,
I'm waiting for you here.

For My Lawyer, My Banker, My Boss, and My Wife

Ḵaadaasháan jiyís

When salmon swim to taste the final stream,
the time has come to sing a glory song;
in kindness we will gather in a dream
and talk of days when one and one was strong.
We think that sorrow names the riverbank.
We think of times in terms and tones of loss.
The weight will press, compress, erase and blank
the lives, at first, they roll, they rift, they toss.
And of this life the fry so subtle drank
before the leaves did fall and ground did frost;
so many laughs, stories for which we thank:
for joy, my Auntie's life and love, star-crossed.
    Our wealth, our will, our strength call unity
    and grace renames the shore eternity.

Dreaming of My Time

I carve my name in Cedar,
because I like the smell of
tradition in my fingertips.

This is how we do it,
a dream once told me,
this is how we tell our stories.

I carve my name in Cedar,
rolling life between fingertips,
feeling for creation.

This is how we do it,
a teacher once told me,
this is how we feed our children.

I carve my name in Cedar,
because I can feel designs
bursting from the grain.

This is how we do it,
Raven once told me,
this is how we heal our people.

Dear Father

June 16, 2015

A year ago you left us behind,
your jokes, your deviance, your rage, your strength.
This is a rock and roll life.
All these stories of your rebellions,
and sometimes my children don't listen:
 I see you through their faces,
  all these days of forever while you might still be here.

Shall we keep it casual?
We could talk sports no matter what the situation,
in fact that was the default:
keep the legs moving so the mind doesn't stain.
A bruise on the spirit tells its own story
 and we reach the one year mark,
  we can begin letting go.

The Bay blew up with championships.
Giants and Warriors and colors I see
you in today, except for your Browns,
who evade a heavenly touch.
You are always with me, and I with you,
 and what rage can counter
  the stupidity of this world?

I am sorry you were alone.
Did you know I was in for a lonesome time?
The brightness of these babies can gauze
the long string of suffering,

these bombs called churches twist my guts,
    I see them through your face
    and want to burn a thousand forts.

You stood up to the beast.
You believed in nothing,
You became it all for us.

Aх Tláa Aх Een Akanik Noojín[*]

Kaxwaan Éesh Jiyís (for George Davis)

aх nák yeegoot aagáa хat galtíshch,
    léelk'w,
    wáa sá k'idéin yéi yisaneiyín
    aх ḵusteeyí,
    aх yéi jineiyí.

i hídidé хwaaḵooх aagáa haa yoo х'atángi
    ḵa haa yéi jineiyí
    k'idéin át kaawadaa,
    wé ch'áagu ḵáax'u
    has du daat yoo х'atula.átgin.

tleidahéen áwé gunéi i náḵ yaa nхagút,
    aagáa хáan keeyaneek:
    aх tláa aх een akanik noojín:
    ch'as tula.aan ḵa ḵusaхán
    i téiх' tóo yéi na.oo!

i dlaak' tin, Shaksháani, yéi jitooné noojín,
    gunalchéesh áwé хaan keeneegí,
    daat eetéenáх sá haa yatee,
    wáa sá aхalхéis' has aguхsakóowu
    wé Yaa Ḵoosgé Daakeit aayí.

haa jeeх eeteeyín,
ách áwé kei guхlatseen, léelk'w.

---

[*] An English translation of this poem appears on page 99.

Du G̲oojí Yinaadé

K̲eixwnéi k̲a Xwaayeenák̲ has du jiyís[*]

"The brown bear picks an apple,"
I say dramatically in the produce section,
Dick Dauenhauer looks up, puzzled, then smiles,
this man who I have shared journeys with,
this teacher who calmly explained that we
are working in the most difficult language in the world.

"We are his potatoes now."
I proclaimed during an academic memorial
while thinking about the high staccato of his laughter,
and the depth of his love for Nora,
a halibut hole and a half of chasing one another
in poems, grammar, immersions, and outdoor adventures.

"I better comb my hair,"
Nora says after I ask to record her speaking Lingít,
this woman who sat on the other side of technologies
and produced hundreds of hours of language collection
that keeps us linked hand in hand,
beneath the forest floor she connected the root systems.

"Ch'a wéit'aa ax̲ een yéi jiné,"
she said when Keiyishí came to visit and asked who
Nora was working with now, and I feel sorrow and a sense
of fulfillment in knowing that we keep the recorder going,
and the translation work and the mountains of papers
that we hope will shine lights on the paths to speaking.

---

[*] For Nora Marks Dauenhauer and Richard Dauenhauer

"It's your turn,"
she says to me when I ask her to translate the words
of her mother's mother's father: Ḵuchéin Frank Italio,
who was probably ninety when he was recorded
in the 1950s, which means he was born in the 1860s,
and we work on his powerful stories a century and a half
after he was born.

It is this moon.
It is this eclipse.
Raven turns her head, towards her wolf,
they leave a mountain of work, which we ascend alone,
but hand in hand now that they cleared an ancient trail.

I close my eyes,
take a deep breath,
and continue our ascent.

Coyote Song III

You think you know what you see;
    eyes lie like thieves in a box;
    rocks & spiders all know
    I take their forms, breathe storms
    across the leveled landscape.

  Close your wandering illusions,
    weakened claw of a scorpion.

  Release your embrace of the serpent
who intoxicates death.

  We are living stories and
    crushing laughter.

  We are dying songs
    wanting more.

    It is about time you came
      home, my child.

G̲agaan X̱'us.eetí

Coyote Song IV

And yes, I am the salt of the earth,
I made the cactus bleed forever.
My claws imprint sand with story,
I level mesas with death eyes.

And yes, there is time for rebirth,
I made the night sky fear isolation,
My teeth hollow canyons, cut jagged bone,
I reduce boulders and birth in my song.

And yes, I am waiting for my children,
I made them hard as sandstone,
eternity in crumbling masses:
They sing a song once forgotten,

rebuilding landscapes in the
ecstasy of survival.

Corbin James

You and me and a pane of glass,
I see my younger face, masking a sorrow;
pumpkin jumpsuit amongst fog walls,
give us some fucking color already.

You and me and a pane of glass,
wasn't long enough I raised you—
now we pendulum lion's teeth,
reduce to silence & muffle & farther away.

You and me and I cannot feel,
handshake or hug in the vise of corrections
my time a sliver of yours, among boils,
infections, and touch nothing.

You and me and a closing bell.
Mother is in hell with her hangover.
Longing for younger days, I stand, leaving
my hope behind, leaving it for you.

Ḵuxdeinú

for Derick Burleson

Some of the days were all absence,
as the winter tilt pushed us towards the ledge
where sunrise and sunset were only separated
by a brief midday.

Tlax̱aneis'

Jilk̲atéet Marion Dennis Madden

The kingfisher is either looking at me or away.
Between dusk and twilight the lines soften and run together.

There is a knot in the tree where all my thoughts reside;
a shadow in aging cottonwood,
beginning to freeze even as a pretend season gives way to the
    thaw:
"The cold is coming, son, the day when I let go of your hand."
    I never wanted to see you this way,
    I never even thought about a time to release.

"She is walking with the ancient ones."
It was all I could say to my big brother, over the phone, in the
    night,
it was all I could do: reach out to all corners of the known
    world,
in one instance I am a child again, protected beneath a
    powerful wing.

The kingfisher is too far away.
I think I know the shape, but my eyes fail me at this distance.

Sometimes we know when we are alone,
even when surrounded by love and growth
the moments turn into themselves,
an eddy where the salmon used to gather.
    I thought at one time I had the strength.
    I thought at one time I knew where to go.

My grandmother once dreamt of a hill,
her two sons played happily but would not look her way,
her husband's parents were with them, looking back at her,
over the distance, letting her know her time had not come.

The kingfisher is gone when I look back,
but why do I feel like it is in my cupped hand?

Onion Bay—Kodiak, Alaska

Explore the territory of other creatures
where energy exists thousands of years
unshaven, untroubled, unbroken.

Everything becomes visible in stillness,
power invades the senses in a spectacle—
    soft patches of moss and mud,
    distant bird whistle and squirrel chirp,
    all pushed by a nudging breeze.

Wide imprints dent the cool
slick edges of a riverbank,
accompanied by those of a small child
still learning the inherited territory,
    practicing tactics of survival in
    a homeland mother calls her own.

If Only in Dreams

In youth I could fly
    away from the hills of turmoil
    and caress the motion of the wind
    with a grace that left my world behind.

Then there was that discussion
    which I had dreamt before,
    and I tore into my mind to find
    the forgotten words
    that may have predicted suicide.

And finally, last night,
    a relative tossed pictures
    to the earth and spoke
    in a language to which
    I am an infant and
    her words were clear to me.

Postcard to My Younger Self

Don't forget to live your dreams.

There are ways to get
   behind the sun.

There are times to crawl past
defeat and the pain will
make you strong.

And the way will be there
   never clear.

And the way will be there
   waiting for you here.

And These Icy Waters

As we drove towards the shore—éiḵde—
I kept thinking about how gray the water was,
the tide rolled like two interlocking hands.
   Aanchgaltsóow: the village that migrated.

It was January, and the air was 20°.
A decade prior our uncle Gaxtlein prepared us
for the water: Don't smile. Don't be fast. Endure.
   Think of everything you don't want and leave it.

The first steps make me exhale—it's needles,
a cold that bites itself in its effort to hold on to you.
The gray of the sky is a lighter tone of the same hue.
   Villagers moved the rocks to make a sandy place here.

Once, twice, three times, but I cannot make the fourth.
When I no longer feel my feet I cannot trust my steps,
but Lyle is in for the fourth: he is the last of us.
   Think of everything you want to be and become it.

The waters are our strongest source of strength,
and spirits always recognize those who fast.
Even in loss we can think of ways to give up more.
   The salt is a rock inside our spirit.

Earthquake Poems

RIDE WITH A SMILE

The dance of the world
just jumps onto the stage,
muscle memory and live step.

I watch the performance,
fascinated in how the parts
move and power feeds all.

These trees have a new song,
though, and when the heart
stills I realize it was a fun ride.

This wonderful world, all power.
This infinite moment, all motion.

Kéet Goosh Áwé
Haa Daa Yéi Yatee[*]

Ḵájaa Darian Twitchell

Kéet Goosh.

Tleidahéen áwé i tláa ḵa ̱xat Xuniyaadé wutuwaḵooҳ,
yaakw tlein yíkt áwé uháan, i shátҳi dlaak' ḵa i sáni teen,
Tlaҳ haa káa awdigaan.

Ch'a yákw áwé wutusiteen wé kéet ҳáa.
Yéi áwé haa ḵusteeyí: kéet gadustínni
has du kaadé kandulgátch áwé gánch.

Haa ҳ'éit aywóo!

Ḵaa ҳ'aҳwawóos' wé gánchgaa.
Héen kaanáҳ kaҳwligátch áwé wé gánch
ḵa has du yáade ҳwaashee kéet sheex'í.

Nás'gi aa wutusiteen, gwál kéet tláa ḵa kéet éesh,
áwé has du yádi du ée has awlitóow aadé s ḵunoogu yé
wé Kéet Ḵwáani.

Kei uwatán.
Shuxw'áa aa tlaҳ kínde.
A ítҳ.aa ḵúnáҳ kínde,
has du yátx'i ch'as ch'a yéi gugéink'.

_____
* An English translation of this poem appears on page 100.

A lú kei wjit'áx̱'.
K'idéin akaawa.aak̲w,
k̲a wáa sá haa toowú kligéi a kaax̱
kei wtuwa.íx̱' sagú tin.

Walk through This World with Me

Holding your hand,
I watch intently,
every expression
and breath labors
against the weight of loss.

G̲agaan X̲anyádi

Coyote Song V

You think you know what you hear;
    Changing Woman breathes death over lies
    huddled and hiding beneath boulders,
    I take their suffering,
    whisper death
    rattles over echoing canyons.

Feed your doubts to the river;
    Sunlight burns to roots our despair.

Savage thought flies with Raven,
    who denies the serpent song.

We are etched desert winter
    and thirst for song.

We echo survival and harvest
    dust, ash, terror.

    It is about time to save
    home, my child.

Cutting the Fog

. Headlands Center for the Arts in Marin County,
ancestral lands of the Coast Miwok

The spiritual creatures keep coming by for visits here,
    Aasgutuyikkeidlí* looks back over its shoulder,
    K'ákw† flies over without a single sound,
    Yéil‡ emerges from the brush in front of my footsteps,

A friend once told me about combating loneliness:
    she wept to the river and asked someone to come help.
    Raccoon came up beside her and sat down,
    was still until she felt better and then left.

---

*   Coyote
†   Barred Owl
‡   Raven

Release

There is the knuckle that bore the burden of loss,
weathered and marred by days and nights at sea,
labor's thick lines, like etches of wood grain
that darken with years of use.

Touch of a staff to the floor signals ritual,
cry songs stain every corner of the room,
quiet has left the village streets as cars
line their edges, new posts for village dogs.

An old man's feet shuffle, he will be the last.
He should be tired, but the strength in his voice
is thick with method, reflects speakers of the past.
He is a river for the voice of his uncles.

Four people stand together, look to each other,
strength. Hand over hand they grip the staff,
the room filled with people have just shed their
final tears and above the sobs, it begins.

Yee gu.aa yáx̱ x'wán!

The chant bellows, repeats, is four,
the shift, ceremony, they turn the tide.
These are our old and our new traditions,
a child will stand in the name of his uncle.

Dark Skin and the Betraying Uncle

The tide and the shore,
in the miles that separate,
there is a blossom

of starfish and kelp,
black seaweed decorating
boulders that dip in

the high tide and bask
in the ebb, under moonlight
or heat of the sun.

A rock contains sea
lions, belching a song,
legendary strength

decorates the land
this tiny island where a
name became hero.

Skin darkened by fire,
a nephew disowned by his
uncle, such betrayal.

We now know the true
meaning of strength, it is not
in one, but us all.

Earthquake Poems

GRATITUDE

In some moments,
a minute lasts forever,
the fear stretches out
to all corners.

My thoughts keep returning,
a cycle of quakes that
rupture the daily cycles:
coming, returning.

As I came out on the other side,
the world had shifted.

The moments were gone,
then returned, and I waded
into a delicate grasp

of knowing that I still
had all.

The Times and Ways It Goes

I am standing at the shoreline.
Water cascades up, and over,
telling of a time we soaked here
for strength. The water. The water.
A story was once told of a boy
who became one with the salmon
because he insulted his food,
abandoning sacred for a richness
presumed privilege. And waste,
that ticking clock on the wall
laps over toes disconnected.
One small step forward.

No food here. Not for a little while.

The glorious await on the other side,
but not in patient stillness, not in
a silent anticipation of our arrival,
but in tireless hope that we somehow
carry on, with all those battered pieces
of what we once were and ever knew.

My tongue is growing back into a
moldable figure, the end just might
be capable of traversing the distance
and bringing treasures here, anchors
against the merciless gale.

I have learned to see no enemies, but
only the path of love, for people, an
unescapable unity that seems so lost
in this world, where copies beget copies,
where everyone walks by a young girl
dying in the streets, where this man can
brag again about raping our women.

We tell the story, over and over again,
waiting for the right parts to change.

Nanook Sweats

I am the wearer of the original fiber optic,
my skin thick, the color of absence.
Banish those thoughts of a Coca-Cola education
for I am the eater of children, women, and men alike
and in this there is no barbarism,
and in this there is no cruelty,
for all who stand upon land in my house
can name themselves, quite simply, prey.

I welcome you and your great knowledge
back into the circle with the familiar crunch,
a femur between my jaws releases sweet marrow,
and we can journey back to a time when there was order,
for in your chaos the journey leads to the waters edge,
closer and closer each time to the end of the beginning.

Those who met me on my ground,
in my method, the one that churns my heart,
adorn my children's anatomy and breathe connection—
beyond the brutality of denying the circle,
carve my image into the collection of all colors
shape me in transformations of their heroes
until we are, as we have always been, one.

But those days wander into the subconscious,
and children will be born wondering why their heart
already is aching, and men will destruct for defiance,

women will web together the synthetic and layer upon layer
will enclose the unborn into nothingness.
I am absence, presence, strength,
step strongly into an eternal sunset.

X'áas[*]

Chukateen is leaving this world,
Her lungs are filling with water
—they say.

Not long ago she shared with us . . .
    Ax éesh yéeyi haa yamsakaayín:
    a yík wudushk'áatl'i yaakw
    tlákw de x'áasde nakúxch.

We send videos to each other
through the hands of Shkooyéil.
He makes sure she exits through dialogue,
as do all who cup her words,
the river rolling of our language.
    My father used to tell us:
    a boat full of silence
    drifts quickly towards the waterfall.

It's crushing.
The deafening loss.
We give up without a battle cry.
    Ch'u uwayáa k'eikaxwéin
    héide yaa has shunay.át
    aadé haa yoo x'atángi ka haa kusteeyí
    daax' yéi jiyné yé.

These were her last words,
which I cannot translate
because you must run to them.

---

[*] An English translation of this poem appears on page 102.

Ode to Tlingit

I.

Silly boys, silly girls,
how am I supposed to weave
tales of your doings as you,
instead of soaring, dumpster
dive and chatter singsong
rubbish morn?

Hop and peer, let me clear
my throat and think of where
to begin. Maybe they know,
this good audience, about your absent
color, your chameleon call?

That White Man, leading tourists to
FalseLand, asked Mom if you are
like an Angel. To this second helping
of questions I revealed the time
you ate Deer through the anus.

Angelic.

Beak for no blade, hide high in the trees,
mob a blue spruce. That throaty caw pulls at me,
I whisper your name—Yéil. Question your being
with an equally guttural tongue.

II.

The surface of the little lake,
now frozen over, I thought to drill
a hole for fishing, place my ear over
and see if I could hear tiny bubbles.

Store the mouth shut, a lip
blood-cracked from the backhand
that imposes a strict mantra:
Speak English or die.
Speak English and die.
Speak.
English.

There are salmon in the water,
silky shapes trapped beneath ice,
light that shimmers off their scales toss
rainbows in a cold green algae-bottomed pond.

Tiny bubbles. They rise from these
creatures divine, waiting for curious young
to cut the thickness that separates identity
from life on the sea's shore.

Life around this place is called
hemlock, douglas fir, alder, cottonwood,
cedar red and yellow.

III.
Stillness!

You are rocks now within the river's churn,
that is what you must become,
what we call Raven's luggage,
let nothing move so you can absorb
that open-mouthed roar containing
secrets I cannot tell you.

Later, in the silence, the river rush
will be a whisper that appears a moment
before your words.
You can barely make them out
over the crunch of herring eggs on
hemlock branches, citrus fish
complimented with a fermented grease.

Somewhere inside a spirit wants to crack skulls,
the cops barely care that your women
will be raped, murdered,
and beneath large beach rocks is another White Man,
a soft-shelled crab scurrying from your sunlight eyes
with deeds clutched in dark gray claws.

These diversions are killing
your Grandmother's tongue,
a stone wheel slowly smashing the soft
fleshy meat pulled from its clamshell.

IV.

Grandmas laugh while laying out berries—
—blue, soap, salmon, thimble, neigóon—
when asked how to say "teddy bear" they smiled
"that teddy bear will kill you" and for the first time forgot
that sacred words are dying, that songs are drifting
from meaning and connection to mere sounds.

In Lḵoot the waters are needle-cold,
in a low fog the clouded sky reaches
down to clutch the land, digging in long
fingers, hiding mountaintops.

A group secludes themselves,
the jackhammer and worldwideweb
cannot rattle on and entice in this camp
where every meal is a ceremony, where art is
perfected through imitation, living as
a minority in a nation of bear and salmon.

High atop a birch, beyond the view of tourist herds,
far from marshals of environmental law and management,
a solitary one pulls a feather the color of absence,
lets it spiral down into the thick river,
where traumatized adults can giggle like innocence,
where every word feeds lost and lone spirits departed.

Forever is best pronounced in a guttural tongue.
Ch'a tleix̱.

Ḵudé Kdagoot

Ḵaaldaaḵeit Debra Ann Carltikoff

Mother, you had passed that point where you could speak.
The sickness was spreading through your body, you had told
    me,
and now it was eclipsing life and concealing you from us.
You are the corona. You are the darkness in the center.

I reached across an ocean to hold your hand,
gave my own salt water to the land and sea and skies.
I did my best to answer those hard questions about dying,
the old people shared ten thousand years of gain and loss.

My sister said you could no longer form sentences.
You were blind. I questioned every single thing in life.
But when they put the phone to your ear,
all I could think of was: Hi, Mommy.

Oh Lance.
Oh son.

Your love cut through the fog
and you are holding my hands as if
they are fuzzy little ravens in a nest.

Maybe we have all day now.
The terrors of this world are shadowed
and we stroll across the diffraction.

« Ch'a yá lingít'aaní kát iguxlatéet. Tléil wáa sá ikgwanei » yóo
    ayawsikaa.*

I said those words to you, over and over.
I sang all of the powerful songs I had learned.
This was your big journey, and we had prepared for it
    together.
On the last day, I stepped into the water.
Tortoises rested on the sand, towards the setting sun.

Wheels hit ground in Alaska.
I turned on my phone.
It rang that very second.
My sister had the confirmation.

"You will just float over the world. Nothing will happen to
    you," he said to her.

That was Raven.
When the world was flooding he instructed his mother.
He shot a black duck and told her to walk into its skin.
She became that bird who tells us where the salmon are.

You live in my dreams.
I remember when I saw your face so clearly,
we were driving around lost.

---

* From Kaasgéi Susie James in her telling of the First Birth of Raven.

I could not stop watching you,
thankful you came back.

It never mattered where we were going.

Tlax̱aneis' Shakeech'eení

Oh my dear brother,
can you see me on the shore
calling out to the endless waves:
Come back. Come back. Come back to me.

You are in my home again.
I put walls around you,
bounced checks around town
to get you a board game, a football.

I'm twenty years old and trying to raise teenagers.
But life gives no mercy to excuses,
and I see my failure to connect and to hold on.

—

Oh my dear brother,
we went to the place where you went out
raining bullets.

A raven is on the telephone pole,
calling out to us over and over and over,
but I know I missed the moment.

Láx' Haa Kináa Wdikeen

Pick your poison tell me what you do
Everybody gon' respect the shooter
But the one in front of the gun lives forever,
(The one in front of the gun forever)
—*Kendrick Lamar, "Money Trees"*

Sometimes I watch herons,
in front of us, guardians of the land.
    —when they fly, we know it's time to go.

Baby brother. When was it I stopped seeing you?
In a photo you hide your face behind a basketball,
I can't put myself there next to you.

When I came up for you and your sister, we were loading
the car and our sister's boyfriend came flying down the
road, started fighting with a crew of guys who followed.

I was able to keep you from that shit, but then gave up;
who is ready to raise teenagers when they are barely
    pushing leaves themselves?

Maybe that's just what I tell myself.

We had you on the phone during mom's funeral.
I had you in pumpkin suits, sitting next to me,
    —when they fly, we know it's time to go.

Sometimes I watch these herons,
«Yéil Éesh»* is how they were called at one point.
They blend with landscape, timeless in their work.

The news showed a truck with the door open,
cases all over, the area taped off,
    it haunts me now and forever.

I wanted to name you "head feather of the kingfisher"
Tlax̱aneis' Shakeech'eení. Someone laughed at me
about it, made a joke for the world.

But there is nothing here but you, my baby boy,
the one I tucked once under my wing,

    but failed.

You and me and these birds forever.

---

* Raven's Father

The Many Cycles of Raven

A FRAGMENT

Kaxwaan Éesh. Shaksháani.

These two Ravens sit with me,
another Raven,
we listen to a Thunderbird
who was recorded in 1952,
when these two elders were twenty-five.

Kuxaanguwutaan

She is one who came among us,
recorded the deepest of our language
on a wire spool stored inside a scotch tape
canister, this tiny box of immense wisdom.

Kuchéin

The master orator left a long path
for his descendants to follow,
and we go one line at a time,
wires cross the kitchen table
in this small trailer that has become
a place of transformation.

Yéil Yú

The White Raven. So many names
and so many stories, yet there is really

no clarity on what happened and how.
When time stretches back far enough,
everything is echoes and shadows
leading somehow towards this moment.

Ḵaayeekoox̱éik

The cycles of Raven have been recorded
over and over, the wheels of tapes and wires
winding and winding as the series of adventures
unfurl—these fiddleheads of late spring that
open the door to fresh flavor.

Yet only one remembered the name:
Raven's Mother, the one who was crying
because her brother killed her children.
Maybe her name means "Paddling Along Below the People"
but these things often escape translation.

Shukalx̱úx̱s'

"There he goes again!" Shaksháani says as we
enjoy the set up, this smooth talker who will
get his way and find methods of making sure
that he gets what he wants and the poor people
are cared for, it's selfish and selfless at the same time,
but it's also not so simple.

Ch'a yá lingit'aaní kát igux̲latéet

Raven said to his mother, "You will just float
upon the world." I shared these words with
my mother, whose life was being consumed
by a great illness, a flood of endings.

Tléil wáa sá ikgwanei

You will be okay. You will be okay.
"Just head south, Mother." That is what people
told me in case you find yourself on the other side.
Neither of us know, but she gave me life
so I give her all the signals I can to help.

Ch'a yá lingit'aaní kát igux̲latéet

All these stories that cycle up and through,
the little arguments about the details and the many
different versions of what happened and where,
what did he steal and what did he keep and what
did he give away.

Tléil wáa sá ikgwanei

The warm ocean laps my toes on the last days
in Hawai'i, and I chant over an ocean that unites us,
divides us into you and me and connects us

into a single journey across worlds,
back in the moment when you held me,
back in the moment I was there when
they put the device in your chest.

Ch'a yá lingit'aaní kát iguxlatéet

I keep singing to you.
I keep telling you these lines.
I keep you in the story a little longer.
Your vision has left you and sister says
most of the words don't make sense anymore.
We are close.

Tléil wáa sá ikgwanei

I keep singing to you.
These little death lullabies that I've picked up.
Calling the end back to the beginning.
I say to you, "Hi Mommy," and you call my name,
you call me son one more time.

The end keeps coming back to the beginning.

The Long Walk

for Sol Jackson Neely

I knew it was time to conspire once
I walked into your office, uninvited,
and closed the door.
We had trickster plans to untangle.

Sometimes we talked in hushed
voices, because there were active forces
of resistance around us, the systemic
fortresses that blocked out change.

And I'm back on Etolin Street in a small house
with you, your wife, your child, my wife, our children,
and our downstairs neighbor Joe,
we were connoisseurs of grass jewelry.

Spider takes a walk on eight legs,
Raven lands in a tree nearby and makes a solitary
call, eastward, southward, a wind that rocks
small boats in a tight channel.

My friend, who shall I plot with now,
as we deconstruct the hollow pillars of
colonization, replacing them with walls
stuffed with medicines and love and courage?

Spider takes a walk on eight legs,
over a body of water and into unknown lands,
Raven flies out of the tree and into the
next narrative, which we write together.

Homecoming

I am from
the hard-cored place:
Áa Wushigágu Yé,
where the heavy hands of the prospector
did their best
to make our ancestral lands
the place of their birth.
    —colonizer—
You can be here and be with us;
you can be here and be a tourist;
only one has knowledge of place.
    —unifier—
One time a friend asked with compassion:
can't we just be one?
I asked which one we would be.
If it's the Lingít-speaking one,
then count me in.
    —terrorizer—
I am from the bottom of a bottle.
The smell of bourbon tells me
it's time to run
from a father who is eaten by demons.

He told me once,
in the last days before his big journey,
in the last conversation I ever had with him,
about that place.

A Catholic boarding school,
where they kept taking his sister down
and beat his face in when he tried to stop them.
A child against tyranny
grows into a giant of a man
who collapses inward.

"That's when I gave up on it all,"
he says.
"I didn't say 'I love you' enough,
but I didn't know I was supposed to,
and I do."
        —survivor—
I am from the wooded place:
trees that intertwine their fingers
below the surface,
on a windblown mountaintop.

We will not topple.
The snow melts at the end of the harshest seasons.

Coyote Song VI

I laugh at the spinning world—ceremony.
I lodge myself in the belly of monsters—fight for babies.

My song decorates canyon walls—covers mesas like shadows
    at dusk.
My life circle—tumbling the maze of eternity.
My eye the first star—welcoming dusk.
My meals of winter snow, stories and song.

I nuzzle your side in a place untouchable, descend into
    original worlds in chant.
We are blue corn pollen—fragrant cedar tips.
I watched your journey with a true mother's patience.
We are the window in the great eye of the universe—reborn
    and new.

I whispered to my babies before stepping to the worlds below:

Walk in beauty	my child
Walk in beauty	my love
It has become	beauty again
We have made it.	We have made it.
We have made it.	Home.

Glossary

AANCHGALTSÓOW • the Lingít name of Auke Recreation Area

AASGUTUYIKKEIDLÍ • coyote | aas-gutú-yík-keitl-i → tree-forest-in.
(shallow.container)-dog-relational

ÁA WUSHIGAGU YÉ • The Heartwooded Place, the Lingít name for
Skagway

AX • my

CH'A TLEIX • forever

CH'A WÉIT'AA AX EEN YÉI JINÉ • only that one works with me

CH'A YÁ LINGIT'AANÍ KÁT IGUXLATÉET • you will just be afloat on the
waves of the world

DU • their (singular)

ÉIKDE • from the inland toward the ocean

GAGAAN • sun

GAGAAN XANYÁDI • sundog | gagaan + xán-yát-i → sun + beside-child-
relational

GAGAAN X'OOS • a beam of sunlight, referring to the beam itself and
not where it contacts anything | gagaan + x'oos → sun + foot

GAGAAN X'US.EETÍ • in a sunbeam; in a ray of sunlight; referring to the
illuminated space where the sun light contacts a surface | gagaan +
x'oos-eetí → sun + foot-remains/imprint

GAGAAN X'USYEE • where the sunbeam hits a surface, illuminating it |
gagaan + x'oos-yee → sun + foot-below

GAXTLEIN • the Lingít name of Paul Jackon (Lukaax.ádi clan)

GOOCH • wolf

GOOSHDEHÉEN • the Lingít name of Si Dennis Sr (Dakl'aweidí clan)
and also of Kájaa Darian Twitchell (Dakl'aweidí clan)

GUNALCHÉESH! • thank you; I am thankful | "it's not easy to get for
oneself"

HAS DU • them all's

JILKATÉET • the Lingít name of Marion Dennis Madden (Lukaax.ádi
clan)

–JIYÍS • for (to have or to benefit) | jee-yís → pessession-for.(benefit)

ḴAAYEEKOOX̲ÉIK • the Lingít name of Raven's mother

K'ÁKW • barred owl

KASÉIX̲JAA • the birth Lingít name of Kiana Twitchell (Daḵl'aweidí clan)

KAXWAAN ÉESH • the Lingít name of George Davis (T'aḵdeintaan clan)

KEIYISHÍ • the Lingít name of Bessie Cooley (Ḵooḵhittaan clan)

KUX̲AANGUWUTAAN • the Lingít name of Fredrica de Laguna (K'inéix̲ Ḵwáan clan)

ḴA • and

ḴAADASHÁAN • the Lingít name of Paul Wilson Jr. (Lukaax̲.ádi clan)

ḴÁALAA • the Lingít name of Miriah Twitchell (Iñupiaq, Daḵl'aweidí clan)

ḴAALDAAḴEIT • the Lingít name of Debra Carltikoff (Lukaax̲.ádi clan)

ḴAALḴÉIS' • the Lingít name of Kiana Twitchell (Daḵl'aweidí clan)

ḴÁJAA • the birth Lingít name of Ḵájaa Darian Twitchell (Daḵl'aweidí clan)

ḴEIXWNÉI • the Lingít name of Nora Marks Dauehnauer (Lukaax̲.ádi clan)

ḴUCHÉIN • the Lingít name of Frank Italio (Shangukeidí clan)

ḴUX̲DEINÚ • eddy; whirlpool | ḵux̲-déin-ú → return-vicinity-is/are-at

LÁX̲' HAA KINÁA WDIḴEEN • heron flew over us

L TUWAX̲SÉE • the Lingít name of Dorothy Dennis (Lukaax̲.ádi clan)

NÁANII • grandmother (in Haida)

NEIGÓON • nagoonberry

SHAAWATK'É • the birth name of Ava Twitchell (Daḵl'aweidí clan)

SHAKSHÁANI • the Lingít name of Marge Dutson (Ishkeetaan clan)

SHÓOGUNÁX̲ • (at) first; originally; in the beginning

SHUKALX̲ÚX̲S' • calling the end back to the beginning; composing a song to the children of your clan; singing a clan love song that requires a response from the opposite moiety; Raven creating making things happen through hortative verb yelling

TLAX̲ANEIS' • kingfisher | tlaax̲-**aa**-√naa-s' → mold-one(s).(part.i)-√grease/apply.lotion-in.series

TLAX̱ANEIS' SHAKEECH'EENÍ • the Lingít name of Corbin Carltikoff (Lukaax̱.ádi clan)

TLÉIL WÁA SÁ IKG̱WANEI • nothing bad will happen to you; you all will be okay

WOOLNÁX̱ WOOSHK̲ÁK̲ • | wool-náx̱ + wu-sh-√k̲ák̲ → hole-through + perfective-cl.(d,sh)-√land/squat

XWAAYEENÁK̲ • the Lingít name of Richard Dauenhauer (Chookaneidí clan)

YAA KANAGWÁTL YÁ LINGÍT'AANÍ • the world is spinning

YEE GU.AA YÁX̱ X'WÁN! • have strength and courage, all of you!

YÉI ÁWÉ AADÉ YÉI YOO DUDZINEIGI • that is how people do things

YÉIL • raven | can refer to the bird (Corvus corax), the Trickster Raven, or the Raven Moiety of clans

YÉIL ÉESH • Raven's Father, sometimes what a heron is called due to its role in the Raven Cycle

YÉIL YÚ • white raven

–YINAADÉ • toward the area of

YÓO AYAWSIK̲AA • they said that to them

Translations

Little One

Kaséixjaa Kiana Catherine Twitchell

my little one.
precious thing.
you are amazing.
my child.

have strength and courage.
have strength and courage.

sometimes
this world is always difficult.

Our Land
it is shaped like a bad thing
Our Language.

nothing is ours.

Our Land.
Our Way of Life.
Our Language.

but it is inside you,
our hope.

we are going to try, we are going to try again
their thoughts
is what we will become
The Eternal Ones.

you are their courage.

my child.
you are amazing.
precious thing.
my little one.

First Words

Shaawatk'é Ava Renae Twitchell

my child.
my child.

we were looking for you
we were looking for you

there is your mother
that is your mother

I am your father
I am thankful
I am thankful

sometimes
this life is very difficult for us
our language is dying

but with you
it is gaining strength
it is gaining strength

our Lingít identity

we love each other
with our language

we love each other
with our language

I am thankful, I am thankful
that is how it is

My Mother Used to Always Tell Me

Kaxwaan Éesh Jiyís (for George Davis)

you left me behind, and then I am always lonely,
    grandfather,
    how wonderfully you made it
    my life,
    my work.

I went to your house and then our language
    and our work
    flowed well,
    the ancient peoples,
    we used to talk about it.

one time I was starting to leave you,
    and then you told me:
    my mother used to always say it to me:
    just kindness and love
    put it in your heart!

with your sister, Marge Dutson, we always used to work,
    I am thankful you told me,
    what we need,
    how I wish that they would know it
    the things of this Box of Wisdom.

you used to put it in our hands,
that is why we will gain strength, grandfather.

That Is a Killer Whale Fin around Us

Ḵ́ajaa Darian Twitchell

Killer Whale Dorsal Fin.

One time your mother and I were boating to Hoonah,
aboard a big boat, with the oldest sister of yours and your
    paternal uncle.
It was very sunny upon us.

Suddenly we saw a pod of killer whales.
That is how our culture is; whenever a killer whale is seen
people put tobacco down upon them.

Send us something to eat!

I was asking people for tobacco.
I sprinkled it onto the water
I sang killer whale songs to them.

The third one we saw, maybe a killer whale mother and killer
    whale father,
they were teaching their child how to be
a Killer Whale Person.

They jumped out of the water.
The first one up very high.
The following up really high,
their child, though, just a little bit.

It's nose popped up.
It gave it a good try,
how proud we were of it
we shouted with joy.

The Waterfall

Chukateen is leaving this world,
Her lungs are filling with water
—they say.

Not long ago she shared with us . . .
    My former father used to say to us:
    a boat full of silence
    always goes toward the waterfall.

We send videos to each other
through the hands of Shkooyéil.
He makes sure she exits through dialogue,
as do all who cup her words,
the river rolling of our language.
    My father used to tell us:
    a boat full of silence
    drifts quickly towards the waterfall.

It's crushing.
The deafening loss.
We give up without a battle cry.
    It is as if flowers
    you all are leading them this way
    the way, our Language and Way of Life
    you all are working on it.

These were her last words,
which I cannot translate
because you must run to them.